Sociology in Action

Howard Housen

Broward Community College

KENDALL/HUNT PUBLISHING COMPANY
4050 Westmark Drive   Dubuque, Iowa 52002

CONTENTS

CHAPTER 1

Sociology as a Field of Scientific Study

The Social Sciences

The social sciences can be viewed as an umbrella under which six (6) related disciplines that study various aspects of human behavior are housed.

1. Anthropology studies:

   human civilizations.

2. Economics studies:

   production, distribution, and consumption of goods and services.

3.   **Political Science studies:**

The way we govern ourselves.
Government and power

4.   **Psychology studies:**

Individual behavior

5.   **Sociology studies:**

human behavior within contex
of a group.

6.   **History studies:**

the past, past events and
helps to prepare for future

The Natural Sciences vs. The Social Sciences

The Natural Sciences (e.g. physics, chemistry, biology) are called "hard" sciences because they:

"HARD" Facts. Proven before your eyes. Always the same "reaction."

The Social Sciences are called "soft" sciences because they:

"Emotional" and change every day. i.e. attitude.

From Common Sense to Science

Prior to sociology becoming an established area of scientific study, social thinkers at the time relied on common sense to answer social questions. The information however, was not always reliable or consistent. Consider for example, the popular saying, "absence makes the heart grow fonder." There is an element of truth here, but it is equally true that, "out of sight, out of mind" and so is, "if the cat is away the mice will play." A young man therefore, who goes away to test if his lover really misses him runs the risk of being forgotten, or worse yet, have his lover find someone else to play with during his absence.

Can you think of some other conflicting truisms?

The Path of Sociology

Three timely forces propel sociology into the ranks of science. They are:

1. The Industrial Revolution

Agricultural to machine. Wisemen didn't know what would happen.

2. Exposure to other cultures through travel

Explored other countries and where exposed to different expireances they've never had or seen.

(3.) Success of the Natural Sciences

knew now

Profiles in Sociology

Write a brief summary on each of the following sociologists:

Auguste Comte:

Coined the term sociology and launched the positivistic approach to sociology

Herbert Spencer:

Concluded that evolution of society and survival was linked to the ability to adapt.
"survival of the fittest"

W.E.B. Du Bois:

One of the founders of the NAACP where he aplied his theories to empower blacks.

Wright Mills:

Wrote "The Sociological Imagination" and "The Power Elite"

Jane Adams:

Not a sociologist but helped establish Hull House for homeless. Founder of American social work. Won Nobel Prize.

The Sociological Imagination

Definition:

Quality of mind that provides an understanding of and selves within the context of larger society.

Components of the Sociological Imagination:

1. See the general in the specific (particular)

2. See the unique (strange) in the familiar

3. Put the individual in a social context

_____

_____

_____

The Sociological Perspectives

The Sociological Perspectives, (also called paradigms, and approaches) describe ways of looking at society. The three classic perspectives are:

1. Functionalist Approach

The Functionalist perspective views society as a set of interrelated parts, each performing specific functions that keep the society in a state of equilibrium, balance, or homeostasis. Key functions are categorized as:

Manifest: Those functions that are explicit or commonly known, e.g.:

taking your child to school to get an education.

Latent: Those functions that are less obvious, and not easily seen, e g.:

Using school as a babysitter.

To fix society, all a sociologist has to do is find the part that is not performing its functions well. In other words, the sociologist needs to find the **Dysfunctions**.

Explain why **latent** functions present particular difficulties for a sociologist who is trying to identify dysfunctions in a society.

Because they are hidden and not admitted.

2. The Conflict Perspective

The Conflict Perspective focuses on the tension, competition, and change found in all societies. Since the valued resources in a society are never equally distributed, in analyzing a society, a conflict theorist asks two important questions:

◇   What are the valued resources in the society?

◇   Who has most of the valued resources?

The answers to these questions reflect who has the ___*power*___ (power) in the society.

And those with the power will always arrange things to benefit ___*selves*___ (themselves) first.

Give examples of how you see this principle operating in the United States or in your culture.

○ wars to get oil
○ most people running for office have alot of money and use it to campaign, not to do good.

Can conflict be beneficial to society? Explain.

We can learn from it.

3. Symbolic Interaction Perspective

The Symbolic Interaction Perspective looks at the way people act toward, respond to and influence one another in society. Unlike both the Functionalist and the Conflict Perspectives which focus on large scale structures in society (macroanalysis), the Interactionist Perspective is concerned with the everyday events (microanalysis).

Give an example of a:

Macroanalysis focus:

Microanalysis focus:

_____

_____

_____

4. The Multi-dimensional Approach

The Multi-dimensional approach employs all three perspectives to study society, believing that the composite result is more comprehensive than that obtained by any of the three individually.

Which of the preceding sociological perspectives (paradigms) would be most effective in studying how the U.S. society functions? Defend your answer.

_____

_____

_____

_____

_____

_____

Notes:

CHAPTER 2

Doing Sociology

The Goals of Science

Science plays a significant role in our lives because it generates knowledge that is derived from direct systematic observation. Armed with this knowledge, we can predict and control many events in our lives. Simply put then, the three basic goals of science are:

1. To understand

   To have knowledge and grasp concepts.

2. To predict

   Believe and state what will or can happen. From your understanding

3. To control

   Take your understanding and predictions and make something happen.

The degree to which we are able to make predictions and therefore control events is largely tied to our ability to establish a cause and effect relationship between two variables. The relationship can be diagrammed as follows:

The Goals of Science

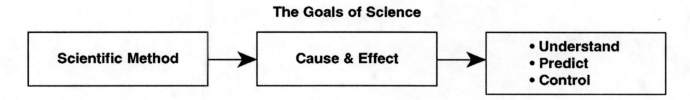

Let's see how this works.

Jeff, a research student, is asked to design an experiment. He selects as his subject, Susie, one of his classmates. His question, "What happens to Susie when she drinks?" To find the answer to this question he got Susie to agree to a series of tests. On day one he gave Susie a measured amount of vodka. After about 30 minutes Susie began to giggle for no apparent reason. He noted this behavior on his chart. Day two he repeated the test and again, in about 29 minutes Susie starts to giggle. This same result was obtained on the third trial. His conclusion, Susie giggles when she drinks.

At a fraternity party, Jeff saw Susie go up to the bar for a drink so he wagered a bet with his friends that he thinks that in about 30 minutes Susie would start giggling. And sure enough, that's what happened. At another party Jeff spotted Susie in a corner crying. She explained to him that she and Allen, her boyfriend, had just broken up. Jeff went to the bar and got Susie a drink, and, in about 30 minutes Susie was up giggling and dancing.

Explain how the three goals of science were achieved in the above story.

°understand - ran tests

°predict - At party saw her drinking.

°control - knew vodka would make her laugh.

The Research Cycle

The following is a step-by-step procedure which scientists follow when conducting scientific research.

A Research Model

Define the Problem
Choose a topic for research.

Review the Literature
Become familiar with existing theory and research on the subject.

Formulate a Hypothesis
State the problem as a testable hypothesis and construct operational definitions of variables.

Choose a Research Design
Select one or more research methods: experiment, survey, observational study, or use existing sources.

Collect the Data
Collect and record information in accordance with the research design.

Analyze the Results
Arrange the information in orderly form and interpret the findings. Confirm, reject, or modify the hypothesis.

Draw a Conclusion
Discuss the significance of the findings.

Posing New Research Questions

Popular Research Methods

1. Survey

The Survey is commonly used when the researcher wants to know people's opinion, feelings, or attitudes (e.g. which of the two major political parties do college students prefer?). Key components of the survey method are:

◇ **Target population**—the group about which the researcher wants to get the information.

◇ **Representative sample**—a smaller number drawn from the target population, whose views are representative of the larger group.

◇ **Random selection**—the method used to select the representative sample. This method ensures that every member in the target population has an equal chance to be selected in the representative sample.

◇ **Questionnaire**—an instrument containing a series of questions that the participants from the representative sample complete and return to the researcher.

◇ **Interview**—one-on-one, face-to-face session in which participants answer designated questions.

◇ **Open-ended questions**—questions that allow the respondents to write in their views on the selected issue. (e.g. What do you think of the Republican party?)

◇ **Closed-ended questions**—questions that have prescribed answers from which the respondents choose (e.g., compared to the Democratic party, the Republican party is a) more conservative, b) less conservative, c) they are about the same).

2. Observation Studies

An Observational Study is an intensive examination of a particular group, event or social process. The task of the researcher is to provide an accurate description and analysis of what actually takes place. The researcher does not in any way attempt to influence the events he or she is observing. There are two basic types of Observational Studies:

❑ **Non-Participant Observation (also called Unobtrusive, or Field Study).**

In this study, the researcher observes the occurrence of events as they happen in their natural setting. The researcher does not participate in the events, and the subjects of the study do not know they are being studied.

Give an example of a Non-Participant study

Doctor secerretly watches a child throughout the day in different situations w/o child knowing.

❑   **Participant Observation**

In this study the researcher becomes actively involved with the subjects he or she is studying, who may or may not know that they are being studied. If the group knows that they are being studied the study is called **Overt Participant Observation**, but if the group does not know, then the study is called **Covert Participant Observation**.

Give an example of:

◇   **Overt Participant Observation**

Living with a family knowing who
you are and what your doing.

◇   **Covert Participant Observation**

An undercover operation.
DRUG BUSTS, pretending to be underage
to drink or catch pedophilles.

Compared to Non-Participant Observation, Participant Observation allows the researcher to get "inside" information that he or she otherwise would not have obtained.

Are there situations however, in which the researcher should not use Participant Observation? Explain.

Yes. when they want to simply
observe the individual in their natural
setting.

3. Experiment

Of all the methods of research, the experiment is best at establishing cause and effect because it allows the researcher to exercise the greatest degree of control over the variables. The experiment can take place in a laboratory under carefully controlled situations or in the field under less artificial conditions. In conducting the experiment, two key variables are identified:

cause

The Independent Variable is the one that causes a change in another variable. This is the one the researcher manipulates to see its effects on another variable.

effect

The Dependent Variable is the one that is changed or affected. Put simply, the Independent Variable acts as the cause and the Dependent Variable is the effect.

Remember the alcohol experiment Jeff did with Susie? What was the Independent Variable and what was the Dependent Variable?

Independent Variable

Vodka (cause)

Dependent Variable

Giggling (effect)

Control Group and Experimental Design

A common design used in conducting experiments is the Control/Experimental group design. In this method, individuals are randomly assigned to either the Control or the Experimental group. The variable the researcher wishes to test (independent variable) is administered only to the experimental group while the other group (Control) gets a placebo.

Let's say I wanted to test the effectiveness of a new pill formulated to cure migraine headache. I would get 20 individuals who are experiencing a migraine attack, randomly divide them into two equal groups and then give those in group 1 the migraine pill and those in group 2 a sugar pill. If after several trials, those who got the pill no longer have a headache while the majority of those who got the sugar still have the migraine headache, then I can conclude that the pill does indeed cure migraine headaches.

In order to declare a cause and effect relationship between two variables, a researcher must be sure that no other variable is responsible for the changes he observes in the Dependent Variable. If a variable, other than the one the researcher is testing (the Independent Variable), creates the change, then this variable is known as the **Confounding** Variable. This situation is most feared by a researcher because he is usually not aware that this variable is the one responsible for the changes he sees in the Dependent Variable. The Hawthorne effect, a commonly used term in research, is a kind of Confounding Variable.

Now write your own definition and example of a Confounding Variable:

A confounding variable is a variable unnoticed by the researcher that could effect outcome.
-eating something that took away headache.

Cause and Effect vs. Correlation

Another important situation the researcher must watch out for is the distinction between **correlation** and **cause and effect**. Take this situation as an example. Every summer, researchers observe that crime rates increase at the same time ice cream sales increase. It would be silly to conclude that eating ice cream causes one to commit crime. Correlation does not necessarily mean cause and effect.

Correlation is written - A & B   Cause and effect is written - A then B

Give an example of correlation:

"J-LO and P. Diddy saw together" in headline w/ a picture of the two being shown.

Now give one for cause and effect:

J-LO & P. Diddy seen together and then J-LO & Ben Aflact broke up.

Measures of Central Tendency

Whenever possible, social scientists use quantitative measures when conducting sociological research in an attempt to enhance objectivity. A popular statistical method used in sociological research is **measures of central tendency**. The three most commonly known measures of central tendency are:

1. **Mean:** The arithmetic average obtained by adding up all the values in the distribution and dividing by the number of cases.

2. **Mode:** The value that occurs most often in the distribution.

3. **Median:** The midpoint at which there are equal number of values above it and equal number below.

If I have a group of five children whose ages are:

4
2
5
3
2

The mean age is: _3.$\overline{3}$_____

The modal age is: _2_____

The median age is: _3_____

What important lesson did you learn about calculating the median?

__put the numbers in order._____

_____

_____

2

2

3

4

5

$5\overline{)16}$ ^3.$\overline{3}$

CHAPTER 3

Culture

There are all kinds of misconceptions about culture. Quite simply, culture is defined as the total way of life of a group of people. Conveniently, we can divide culture in two halves—**material culture** and **non-material culture**.

Material culture includes all the tangible things in the society, such as artifacts, tools gadgets, implements and equipment.

Non-material culture involves all the intangible aspects, including values, norms, language, ideas, beliefs, laws, and attitudes.

These two parts work hand in hand to keep the society in a state of equilibrium. The relationship looks like this:

How Culture Works

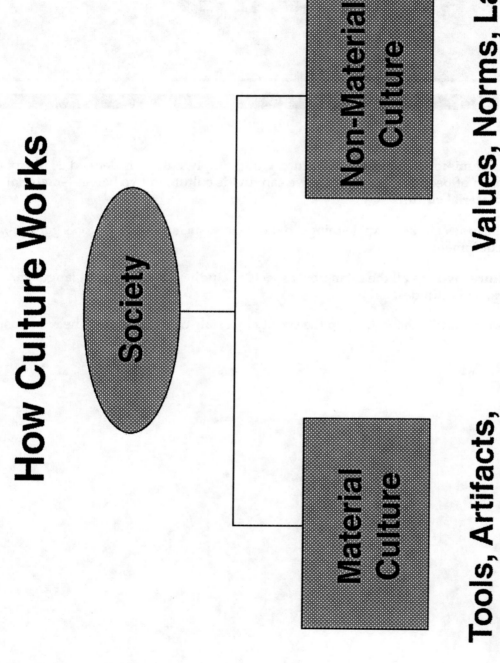

Society

Material Culture

Non-Material Culture

Tools, Artifacts, Cars, TV, Clothes

Values, Norms, Laws, Beliefs, Traditions

And works like this.

For every object on the material culture side, the nonmaterial culture develops a value system which specifies the meaning and use of that object. Every time something new gets introduced on the material side, the nonmaterial culture scrambles to develop guidelines for its integration in the existing value system in the society. This process usually takes time, and sociologists refer to this time lapse as **culture lag time**.

Culture lag time then can be defined as:

The time frame it takes society to get back to an equalibrium.

We will look at this important phenomenon again when we discuss technology as a source of social change.

To survive, a culture must identify a set of behaviors that everyone is expected to follow. These are called **norms**. All norms, however, are not created equal. There are four major types of norms.

Continuum of Norms

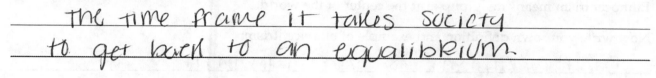

Folkways: Folkways are informal rules and expectations that provide guidelines for everyday living. Write an example of a folkway.

Mores: Mores are serious norms that are considered critical for the proper functioning of society. They usually carry significant moral implications and are seen as protecting what is right and good.

Laws: Laws are codified mores. The society says these expectations are so important that we are going to write them down because without them chaos would reign.

Taboos: Taboos are prohibitions that the society believes everyone should instinctively consider unthinkable and repugnant, e.g. incest.

Why is incest considered a universal taboo?

Because it should be unthinkable

To encourage conformity to and discourage violations of its norms, society utilizes **sanctions**. Sanctions therefore have both a _positive_ (reward) component and a _negative_ (punishment) component.

Eventually, we come to accept our culture's ways of doing things so much so that we think our ways are the best when compared to other cultures. Sociologists call this **ethnocentrism**.

Ethno = my group   Centrism = center

Ethnocentrism means my group is at the center of the world.

Now write your own definition and example of ethnocentrism:

ethnocentrism is an ignorant approch to cultures which makes the assumption that your own is the best.

The opposite of ethnocentrism is **cultural relativity**. How would you define cultural relativity? What's a good example?

Some other opposites:

Subculture:

Counterculture:

Ideal Culture:

_____

_____

Real Culture:

_____

_____

CHAPTER 4

Socialization

How would you answer this million-dollar question?

What we become is predominantly determined by: (Pick one of the following)
our environment *nurture*   our genes *nature*

Defend your answer:

I would say both but if i had to choose one, i'd say enviornment based off my own personal expireances.

The Nature/Nurture Debate

You have just gotten drawn into the age-old nature/nurture debate. Supporters on the nature side claim that it is our biology that has the greatest influence on what we become, while nurture side supporters say it is our environment that is most important. You, like most experts however, think that both together play a key role in the transformation of a helpless infant into a full functioning adult. This transformation is what sociologists call **socialization**, the process through which we develop a sense of self and learn the attitudes, values, and norms of our culture. If this does not happen we fail to develop human traits, as in the case of feral children who are reared without human interaction.

Socialization is defined as:

_____

_____

_____

Personality Development

A dominant pattern of attitudes, feelings, and behaviors that each of us develops, is what is referred to as our personality. It was Sigmund Freud who suggested that the personality has three important components: the id, ego, and superego.

The id:

_____

_____

_____

The Superego:

_____

_____

_____

The Ego:

_____

_____

_____

The Ego at Work

Id ⟵————————————————— **Ego** —————————————⟶ **Superego**

As you can see, the ego serves the important function of keeping both the id and superego in check. What happens if:

The id takes over:

_____

_____

_____

The superego takes over:

_____

_____

_____

Major Agents of Socialization

Agents of socialization are defined as:

_____

_____

_____

They include:

1. The family   4. The peer group

2. Religion   5. The workplace

3. The school   6. The media

The traditional ideal sequence looks like this:

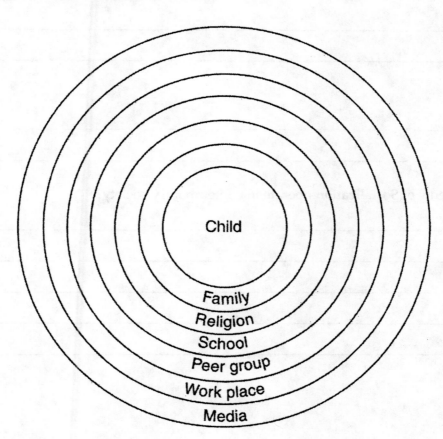

And here is how they work together:

The family

_____

_____

Religion

_____

_____

The school

_____

_____

The peer group

_____

_____

The workplace

_____

_____

The media

_____

_____

How do the Agents of Socialization operate in contemporary society?

_____

_____

_____

_____

Socialization across the Life Course

We do not want to leave the impression that socialization happens only to children because socialization is really a life-long process. To understand this let's look at the life course.

The Life Course

Childhood	Adolescence	Adulthood	Old Age (Death)

As we reach each milestone, we are expected to display the behaviors appropriate for that stage. In other words, society does not expect a two-year-old to behave like a 16-year-old and vice versa.

In many cultures, specific rituals called rites of passages are used to indicate when these markers are reached. Can you identify some that you have heard about or participated in?

_____

_____

_____

_____

Desocialization and Resocialization

Desocialization involves "the unlearning of previous expectations and roles," while resocialization is "learning a radically new set of norms, attitudes, values, beliefs, and behaviors." Both desocialization and resocialization are effectively carried out by total institutions.

Give some examples of total institutions and what each is trying to accomplish:

_____

_____

_____

_____

CHAPTER 5

Society and Social Interaction

Civilizations: The following is a brief overview of key civilizations:

Hunters and Gatherers

- ◇ Nomadic
- ◇ Small population
- ◇ Women gathered berries
- ◇ Men hunted animals
- ◇ Egalitarian

> Division of Labor

Pastoralists

- ◇ Less nomadic
- ◇ Increased food supply
- ◇ Larger population
- ◇ Domesticated animals

Horticulturalists

◇   Less nomadic

◇   Increased food supply

◇   Domesticated plants

◇   Larger population

Agrarian

◇   Use of plow

◇   Increased food supply

◇   Increased population

◇   Created surplus

◇   Specialization

◇   Stratification

◇   Additional institutions

Industrial

◇   Mechanization

◇   Industrialization

◇   Urbanization

◇   Classic institutions in force

Classic Social Institutions

◇   Family

◇   Religion

◇   Education

◇   Economics

◇   Government

Post-Industrial

◇   Information

◇   Service

◇   Highly technological

◇   Addition of Science and Technology Institution

Social Institutions

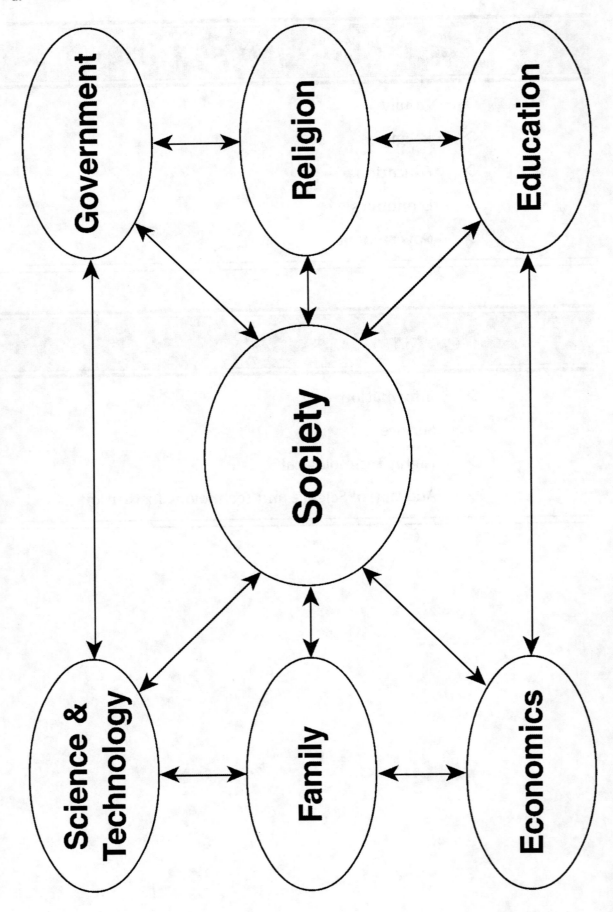

Status

At any given time an individual occupies many positions, in other words, he wears many different hats all at once. For example, the many hats that I wear all at the same time can be diagramed as follows:

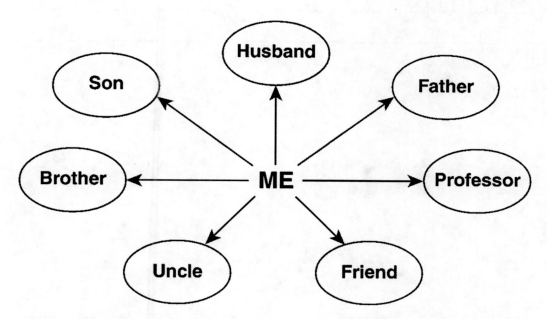

Sociologists refer to these positions as statuses. Statuses that are assigned to us are termed **ascribed**, and those that are acquired through personal effort are called **achieved**. Statuses do not have equal importance. The status that is most highly regarded by the society is said to be a **master status**. In the United States for example, one's profession is generally the master status. For instance, when my students run into me in the mall on a weekend, they do not see me as private citizen X. Rather, they still view me as Professor X.

Now diagram all the statuses you currently occupy and identify which is ascribed, and which is achieved. Then, identify the three most important ones for you right now. The profile of yourself that you just created can be used to uncover important things about you, including who or what is important to you, and possible sources of stress you are now experiencing. You see each status carries specific expectations which we call **roles**. Sometimes these expectations clash with each other. When the clash involves expectations in two or more statuses it is called **role conflict**. If the clash is between expectations within the same status, then it is **role strain**.

Are you currently suffering from role conflict? Explain the situation.

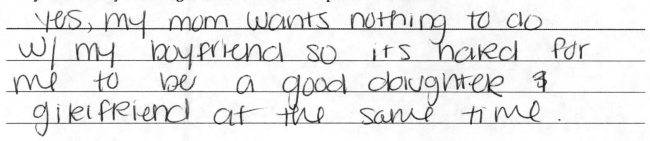

Yes, my mom wants nothing to do w/ my boyfriend so its hard for me to be a good daughter & girlfriend at the same time.

How about role strain?

Yes, I am always caught
between my two
siblings.

CHAPTER 6

Groups and Formal Organizations

In our everyday discussion we refer to any collection of people as a group. But after this unit, you will never make that mistake again because you will know that a collection of people is not necessarily a group. Sociologists have special names for those non-group collections. They are:

Aggregate: An aggregate is a collection of people who happen to be in the same place but who do not interact around shared goals. For example:

people at the bus stop.

Category: A category defines individuals who share something distinctive in common. For example:

All police officers

What is a group? A group is accurately used to refer to a collection of people who interact regularly on the basis of shared expectations and goals.

Types of Groups

Primary Group:

Long lasting. intimate:
family.

Secondary Group:

interaction only over a
period of time:
　　　class

Reference Group:

Sets standards
Gives direction
Role model

In-group:

Strong group allegiance
　　　& loyal.

Out-group:

not part of the in-group.

Group Size: The size of a group significantly affects how the group functions.

A dyad is:

2

A triad is:

3

Group Leadership: Soon after a group is formed, a leader for the group emerges, sometimes formally elected sometimes not. The group leader can use any one of the following dominant styles:

Authoritarian: (Instrumental)

directs and gives order
wants only to achieve goal.

Laissez-faire:

"Let it Be"
Hands off aproach

Democratic: (Expressive)

cares about group input
& emotions.

Although most leaders have a dominant style, an effective leader should be able to employ any one of the styles when the situation warrants it.

Group Conformity involves:

Social Networks includes:

social relationships that link people
to others

Formal Organizations are regarded as:

Structures organized to achieve goals, creates Bureacurey.

CHAPTER 7

Deviance and Social Control

Would you object if I called you a deviant? You should, because a deviant is one who habitually violates society's rules and as a result is labeled.

But at the same time, all of us have committed acts of deviance. There is a big difference between being labeled a deviant and occasionally committing acts of deviance.

Deviance then is:

Over or under conformity to society's norms.

Let's take a closer look at how this works. For most of us deviance means doing something that's bad, but it involves more than that. We'll use the classic bell curve to illustrate this.

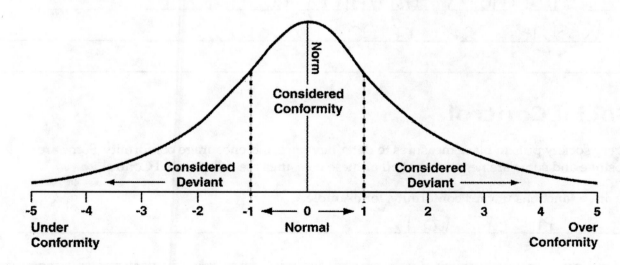

First, let's look at Johnny, who at the tender age of 12 has a rap sheet a mile long. Charges include robbery, burglary, possession of a firearm, assault, and several other offenses. We would all agree that Johnny is a bad boy, and should be punished.

On the other side is Timmy, who is also 12, attends school regularly, completes all his assignments in class, and makes no trouble at school. Timmy's mother instructs him that when he gets home from school he should have a snack, do his homework, and then practice the piano. Timmy does this religiously every day. At 12, Timmy has not shown the slightest curiosity in looking at a girlie magazine. Timmy's dad has become concerned about him and suggested that they should probably take Timmy to see the psychologist. Timmy is not doing anything bad, so why should we be concerned about him? Don't we in fact have some choice names like goody, goody nerd, mommy's boy, for Timmy?

This example illustrates that deviance is movement in either direction away from the norm that society has established.

Types of Deviance

There are two categories of deviance:

Primary Deviance:

violation w/o being labeled.

Secondary Deviance:

violations occuring as a result of being labeled.

Social Control

Every society puts in place measures to deter deviance and encourage conformity. Some are positive and some are negative, but all of these measures are called Social Control.

Positive sanctions reward conformity, for example:

Honor Roll

Negative sanctions punish deviance, for example:

PRISION, community service

Deterrence

According to deterrence theory, deviance will be effectively minimized if negative social sanctions are seen as certain, swift, and severe. There are two major types of deterrence:

Specific Deterrence:

One who is punished so they won't do it again.

General Deterrence:

One who is punished to discourage others from doing it.

Crime and the Criminal Justice System

Crime is defined as:

Violation of a LAW

Categories of Crime

1. Crimes against the Person

Murder, Rape, Robbery, Assault.

2. Crimes against Property

Arson, burglary, Larceny.

3. Victimless Crimes

Gambeling
Prostitution

4. White Collar Crimes

Fraud
embezziment.

5. Hate Crimes

motivated by victums
Race, religon, Sex,
ethnicity

The Police

The police represent the first line of encounter with the criminal justice system in a majority of cases, and in less serious situations it is their decision that determines if we become entangled in the other parts of the system. In other words, the police have this powerful privilege called discretion, as many motorists who have been caught speeding are well aware.

Applying the Law

Carlos, an electronics store owner, had suffered repeated breaking and entering at the hands of a burglar dubbed "Spiderman." The police have failed to apprehend this burglar, so Carlos decided to take matters in his own hands. In the last entry, "Spiderman" had climbed through the ceiling of an adjoining building to gain entrance to Carlos' store, so Carlos rigged up a device, that if tripped, would result in instant electrocution. And sure enough, when Carlos entered his store that morning, there was "Spiderman" completely "fried."

What do you think happened to Carlos when the police arrived and found out what took place?

He was arrested.

Can you think of other similar situations?

What is the basic principle here?

You cant use exusable force when youre not in danger.

The Courts

The Courts basically serve to interpret the law and dispense justice and everyone accused is entitled to his day in court. However, estimates are that 90% of all cases never go to formal trial. These cases are disposed of through **plea-bargaining**.

Plea-bargaining works like this:

Plea guilty to do a less amount of time.

Correctional System

The embraced intent of the correctional system is to rehabilitate those who have violated society's laws. There is heated debate as to whether this happens.

The correctional system uses total institutions such as _prison_ to achieve its objectives of rehabilitation and reform.

One way to measure the success of the rehabilitation effort is by looking at the recidivism rate.

Recidivism is:

Career criminals.

Your Opinion

What do you think should be done to reduce the high crime rate?

It all starts in the home w/ the parents. So I would target parents.

CHAPTER 8

Social Stratification

Stratification reflects a society's system for ranking individuals on a hierarchy. There are four key principles of stratification.

1. Stratification is universal but variable

   All societys are stratified but in diff. ways

2. Stratification persists over several generations

   changes over generations

3. Stratification involves beliefs, not just inequalities

   caste systems

4. Stratification is a characteristic of society, and not merely a function of individual differences

   heirarchy is not b/c of individual efforts

Systems of Stratification

Globally, there are two major systems of stratification. They are **Caste** and **Class.** The features of each are as follows:

Caste System	**Class System**
Status ascribed	Status achieved
Closed	Open
Rigid	Flexible
No mobility	Mobility upward and downward

Here is a diagram of a caste system:

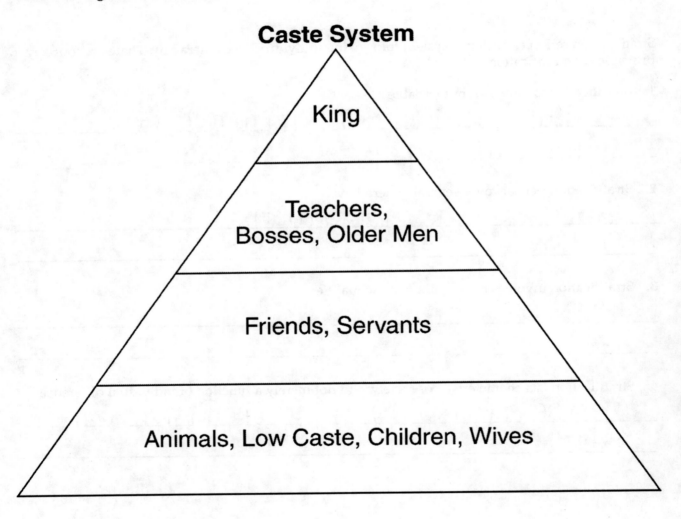

Caste System

King

Teachers, Bosses, Older Men

Friends, Servants

Animals, Low Caste, Children, Wives

In the United States we use the social class system.

In which social class would you put yourself?

_____LoweR Middle class_____

On what basis did you put yourself in that particular social class?

_____I don't live pay check to pay check_____
_____but I don't have assets or excess_____
_____money._____

The US Social Class

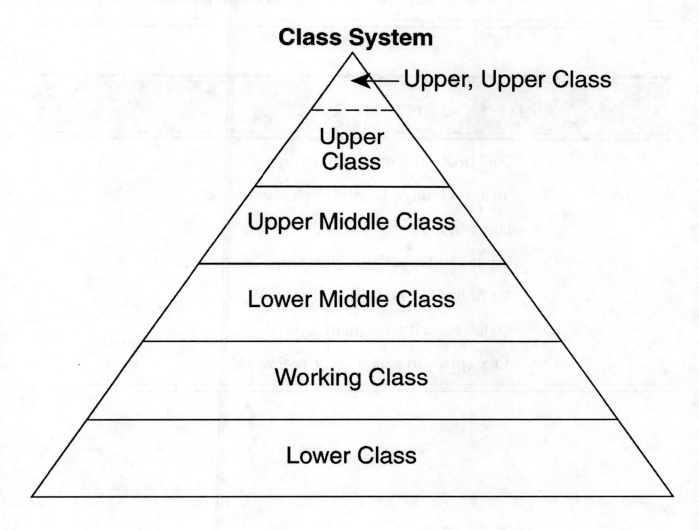

Class System

Upper, Upper Class

Upper Class

Upper Middle Class

Lower Middle Class

Working Class

Lower Class

The Lower Class

◇   Constitute 14-20% of US population

◇   Earn below poverty line

◇   Erratic jobs

◇   Minimum wage

◇   No benefits

◇   Considered disposable, and of no consequence

The Working Class

◇   Constitute 30% of US population

◇   Includes blue collar and clerical workers

◇   Low wages

◇   Unpleasant and dangerous work conditions

◇   No, or limited, benefits

◇   No job security (frequent layoffs)

◇   Takes pride in performing "real work"

The Lower Middle Class

◇   Constitute 33% of US population

◇   Includes teachers, bank employees, midlevel supervisors and salespeople

◇   Earn $30,000–$75,000

◇   Minimal on-the-job decision-making power

◇   Live in modest homes

◇   Try to keep up with the "Jones's"

◇   "Overworked" and "Overspent"

The Upper Middle Class

◇   Constitute 15% of US population

◇   Include corporate executives, physicians, attorneys, and professional employees

◇   Advanced college degrees

◇   Earn $100,000 plus

◇   Live in expensive homes

◇   Drive luxury cars

◇   Active in politics and community affairs

The Upper Class

◇   Constitute 1% of US population

◇   Include CEO's of major corporations, prominent government and media officials

◇   Earn $500,000 plus

◇   Own substantial assets

The Upper, Upper Class

◇   Old money

◇   Original "families"

◇   Blue blood

◇   Proper breeding

◇   Elite

◇   Aristocrats

◇   Membership is ascribed

How Is Rank Determined?

A truck driver earns $100,000 per year, and a professor earns $50,000. Which one would you put in a higher social class?

PROFFESOR

Why?

it is not only based on money.

Although the professor earns half as much as the truck driver, he will be placed in a higher social class because factors other than income are used to determine one's social status. Max Weber is credited for introducing this rating system, which takes into account such factors as:

◇   Income
◇   Education
◇   Occupation
◇   Prestige

This rating system therefore measures your **socio-economic** status (SES).

The Importance of Money

Let's not delude ourselves however. Money is still a major player in the ranking game. To simplify matters, we can look at money under the broad category of wealth, which is divided into two key components:

1.   Income

pay for labor.

2.   Assets

investments, Real estate

In order to become financially secure you have to move from the dependence on just income to the acquisition of assets. With income, you have to work for your money, but with assets, your money works for you. If you don't do this you are likely to end up in **poverty**.

Poverty Is Measured in Two Basic Ways

1. Absolute Poverty:

22,000 POR Family OF 4.

2. Relative Poverty:

based on neighbors
living

Sociologists have added, however, another category called the **feminization of poverty,** which is defined as:

poverty in woman headed
households.

Our social class tells a lot about us due to the fact that it is our social class that largely determines our access to resources, our **life chances.**

Life Chances then are:

Access or Lack of
access to resources

In most societies, there are certain indicators of high status which sociologists call **status symbols.** What are some examples of status symbols in the United States?

- CARS
- Homes
- Clothes

Be careful not to generalize though, because a status symbol in one society may not be a status symbol in another county. Can you think of an example?

- cars here are taxis
there.

We also have to be cautious in the United States due to the fact that most of us have relatively easy access to credit. This allows us to acquire a particular status symbol without having the means to support it.

What's a good example of this?

_____

_____

Mobility within the Class System

As we have indicated before, it is possible to move up or down in the class system and there are two ways of doing so:

1. Intergenerational Mobility:

_____ movement over several _____

_____ Generations _____

_____

2. Intragenerational Mobility:

_____ movement w/ in own _____

_____ life time _____

_____

The following exercise will give you an opportunity to explore intergenerational mobility within your own family.

Intergenerational Mobility

Instructions: Using the following socioeconomic (SES) factors, diagram the social class of four generations in your family, starting with your paternal and maternal grandparents and ending with your children (to be in some cases).

SES Factors

- ◇ **Education:** The highest level reached (e.g. High school diploma)
- ◇ **Occupation:** Type of work (e.g. Accountant)
- ◇ **Income:** Earned annual salary (e.g. $50,000–$60,000)
- ◇ **Prestige:** Level of influence in the community and how he/she is regarded by others

Procedure:

1. Start with your paternal and maternal grandparents. Fill in the information for each of the above factors, then assign a specific social class (e.g. Lower middle) based on those factors.
2. Complete the same information for your parents and assign them a specific social class too.
3. For yourself, project to the future when you are into your chosen career, then complete the information and assign yourself a social class. If you are not currently married, complete the information on your spouse-to-be and assign him/her a social class.
4. Finally, complete the same information for your children (or children-to-be) when they get established in the career that you think they might pursue. Assign them a social class.

Answer the following:

What are you now doing to ensure that you will realize your dreams and positively influence the generations that will follow you? List and explain all that you are now doing in regards to self-development, educational pursuits, financial planning, work experience, volunteer activities, healthy lifestyle, relationships, etc.

Generational Chart

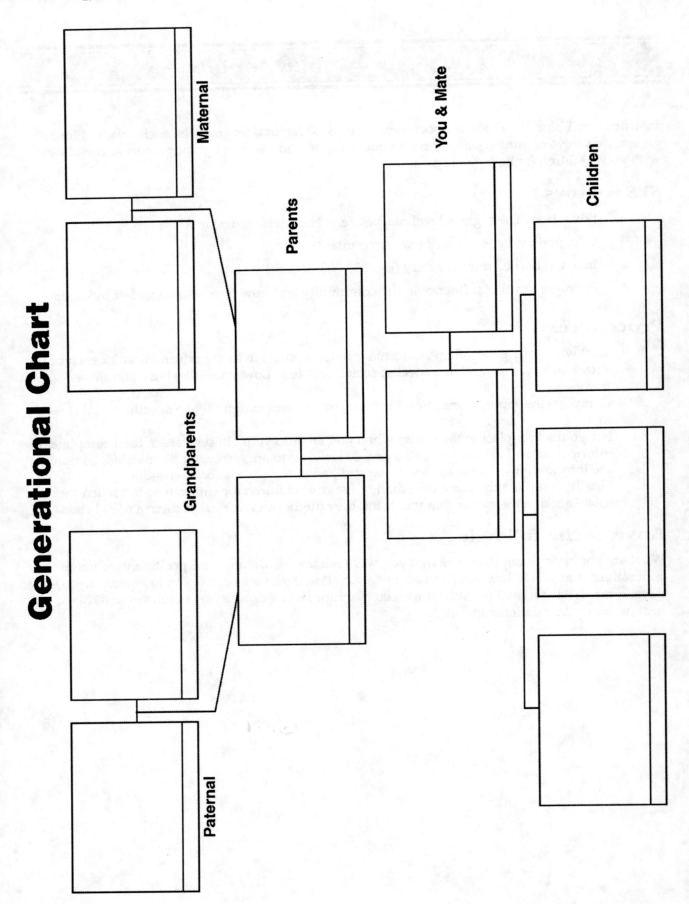

Maternal

Paternal

Grandparents

Parents

You & Mate

Children

CHAPTER 9

Global Stratification

Just as we are able to place individuals in a society on a hierarchy, we do the same thing with nations, ranking them on the basis of wealth, power, and prestige. The ranking is as follows:

High Income Nations (First World)

Advanced industrial economies

Middle Income Nations (Second World)

newly industrialized.

Low Income Nations (Third World)

poor & highly dependant on 1st/2nd world

Theories of Development

Modernization Theory is:

First world developed b/c of embracing tech.

Recipe of Imitation suggests that:

"Do what we aid & you'll be like us."

This won't work because:

1. Geography /colonized

2. dominated manufacturing.

Dependency Theory is:

1st & 2nd keep 3rd dependant through unequal relationships

Dependency is maintained through:

1. Trade Dependency

3rd world sell 1st class goods and we dont do the same.

2. Industrial Dependency

Cheaper labor

3. Investment Dependency

_____

_____

_____

CHAPTER 10

The Inequalities of Race and Ethnicity

A Cultural Journey

Instructions: List below the different groups that are part of your background (heritage). For example, in my background, there is African, German, Chinese, Indian, and British. **What's yours?**

1. Italian
2. Irish
3. Portugese.
4. _____
5. _____
6. _____

When you think of yourself, what do you think of yourself as?

Sicilian

Race vs. Ethnicity: You had only two options from which to choose when trying to decide what group to identify with. You can identify yourself on the basis of race or ethnicity.

Race: Individuals who belong to the same racial group must have similar genetically determined traits that are physically expressed. These include:

◇ skin color

◇ hair texture

◇ body type

◇ slanted eyes

◇ nose and lips

Having said that, let me hasten to contradict myself by saying that race has no meaning bio-logically. What this means simply is that there are no pure races, because human groups have commingled over the centuries and so all of us carry the traits of all the groups. All that happens when it comes to racial features is that the genes that control the above features are dominant genes so these features get expressed. Recessive genes control the other traits that we don't see. Every so often however, a formerly recessed trait gets expressed in one child in a family, thus making that child physically different from other members in his/her immediate family.

How does this happen? Do you personally know of a situation in which this happened?

my father was born w/ red
hair althogh no one in
my family has red hair.

Ethnicity: Individuals who share any combination of the following can be classified as belonging to the same ethnic group:

◇   Nationality

◇   Language

◇   Religion

◇   Culture

Individuals belonging to the same ethnic group do not have to have like features. Therefore you can have a Cuban who is black and a Cuban who is white—different races but same ethnicity. It is imperative therefore that we do not try to identify people on the basis of their expressed physical features.

Since race has no meaning biologically, why has it played such a significant role in this society and around the world? A simple answer is that race has meaning sociologically because society places positive or negative value on the expressed physical features we mentioned above.

Stereotypes

List some common stereotypes of the following groups. (By listing them it does imply that you believe, or use these stereotypes yourself).

Hispanics	Jews	Blacks
dance good here illegaly	cheap nagging	criminals

Whites	Asians	Native-Americans
think they are better cant dance	smart nijas	land lovers hate whites

What are stereotypes?

Assumptions about someone based on skin color or ethnicity.

What have you learned about stereotypes?

they are misreading
and lead to
predjudice & discrimination.

Prejudice is:

Feeling, beliefs or
attitudes towards
another group.

Discrimination is:

Acting on a predjudice.

Types of Discrimination

1. Individual (Personal) Discrimination

based on own
feelings.

2. Institutional Discrimination

unequal treatment w/in social institutions.

Can an individual discriminate without being prejudiced?

Yes ___X___   No _____

The answer is _yes_

Institutional Discrimination:

- morgage companies dont approve Hispanics.

What examples of Institutional Discrimination do you find in the following areas?

Employment:

% of races in work force

Housing:

not selling homes to races/ ethnicities.

Education:

Allowing % of race into a school.

Sports:

_____

_____

_____

The Criminal Justice System:

many blacks usually convicted.

The Media:

way races are precieved.

Pattern of Group Relations: When unlike groups meet the following sequence usually results:

- ⟩ Contact
- ⟩ Competition
- ⟩ Conflict
- ⟩ Dominance

Once a group establishes control, it frequently engages in the what sociologists call **Techniques of Dominance**.

Techniques of Dominance Scale

Genocide	Expulsion	Slavery	Segregation	Assimilation	Pluralism

Genocide is:

dominate a group by extermination

Expulsion is:

removal of group

Slavery is:

Forced Labor w/o pay.

Segregation is:

physical seperation to designated areas.

Assimilation is:

Requiring group to give up customs.

Pluralism is:

Groups co-existing w/ distinctive features.

Apply this process to race relations in the United States:

Hispanics diant want to give up customs, now South Fl is so diverse

The Melting Pot vs. Anglo-Conformity

The Melting Pot concept was believed to be:

never really happened

But what really happened was Anglo-Conformity, which you would describe as:

assimilation

Salad Bowl: The "salad bowl" concept is a way of saying:

"We all mixed together but retained our taste"

What is your vision of the future of race relations in the United States?

CHAPTER 11

Sex and Gender

What would you say are some of the major differences between males and females?

-Genitalia
- Hormones
- masulinity / Femininity

Let's clarify a few terms.

Sexual Identity:

biological differences between male and female.

Gender Identity:

cultural norms on what is masculin and Feminine.

Gender Roles/Expectations:

Society's expectations
on females and males

Gender Socialization:

process by which we learn
gender rules

Sexual Orientation (Preference):

one's preference on a
sexual partner.

Sexual Orientation Scale

Heterosexual	Bisexual	Homosexual

Heterosexual:

attraction for opposite
sex.

Homosexual:

attraction for opposite
one sex.

Bisexual:

Sexually attracted to
both sexes sex.

Transsexual:

Undergone sex
change.

Transvestite:

one who likes dressing
like the opposite sex.

Hermaphrodite:

born with male & female
genitalia.

Sexism:

discriminating against a sex

Sexism in:

Education:

Employment:

Hostile work enviornment

The Media:

girls are sluts while
guys are cool.

Sports:

Bills
Girls dont play Pootball.

The Military:

men dont think women
have their back.

Sexual Harassment occurs when:

Unwanted Sexual
comments OR
gestures are given.

What is your vision of Sex and Gender in the future?

The world is becoming more
tolerant and i feel like
sex and gender will be
messed with.

CHAPTER 12

Age and the Elderly

Gerontology is a fairly new discipline in sociology that studies:

aging of elderly.

The Graying of America means:

U.S population is becoming older.

Life Expectancy:

predicted years a person will live.

Ageism:

belief that those a certian age are inferior to others.

What are some examples of age discrimination?

-not renting to someone old or young.
-not treating one fairly based
on their age

Activity Theory suggests that:

Quality of life is linked to
activity level.

What would be the benefits to society in general, and the elderly in particular, if we implemented the principles of activity theory on a wide scale?

The elderly would stay
active and in turn feel better.

CHAPTER 13

Social Change

Social Change is defined as:

PROCESS through which social behavior, relationships, institutions and systems of stratification are altered over time

Principles of Social Change: There are four (4) major principles of social change.

1. Social change is universal but variable:

World wide but societys change at their own rate.

2. Social change is intentional but also unplanned:

Sometimes orcestrated but natural disasters are unplaned.

3. Social change brings controversy:

    Abortion brought controversy.

4. Social change produces variable consequences:

    Price gauging laws b/c of
           Huricane Andrew.

Sources of Social Change: The following are the primary sources of social change.

1. The Physical Environment:
    - Rivers
    - Resources
    - natural disasters
    All make a group ruged.

2. Cultural Innovation includes:

    Discovery

    uncovering somthing that
    was always there but
    went unknown.
              Beverly Hills Hillbillys.

Invention

combining existing elements to create something new.
- OAR
- proportional to rate of discovery.

Accidental Juxtaposition

accidental inventions

Diffusion

cultural borrowing but is modified to fit recieving culture.

3. Technology

Culture-lag time

time frame it takes society to return to equalibrium after materials.

Technological Determinism

when technology becomes master
and society the slave.

4. Population

The amount of people living
in a given area.

Demography

Study of size, composition,
distribution and changes in
human population.

Population Theories

Malthusian Theory:

As food supplies grows, population
grows geometrically.

Demographic Transition Theory:

1.) ↑ Birth   ↑ death
2.) ↑ birth   ↓ death
3.) ↓ birth   ↓ death

Birth rate (Fertility):

Rate at which birth rises
or decreses

Death rate (Mortality):

Rate at which death rises or decreases.

Fecundity is:

the potential for childbirth.

Rate of Reproductive Change (Natural Increase)

The following equation is used to figure out increases in population due to reproduction.

Birth rate – Death rate = Rate of Reproductive change

Migration:

movment within a country

Net Migration is:

Amount of in-out (a-b=c)

Immigration:

movement outside the country.

Population Mix is:

when different races and cultures live together in given area.

Push/Pull Theory is:

push- move b/o not happy.
pull- pulled by strong forces
            to move.

Support Systems Theory suggests that:

people move to places w/ others
like themselves.

Urbanization occurs when:

From rural areas to
            cities.

A Metropolitan Area (Metropolis) develops from:

A city w/ diff cities
connected. FLL.

Megalopolis is created when:

Several metropolis connected.
      Dade, FLL, Palm Beach

Concentric Zone Theory is used to explain:

White Flight describes the situation whereby:

When one race moves into an area of all "whites" all the "whites" leave.

Gentrification is the process in which:

Renivating areas of decay.

Redlining occurs when:

Area is ran into the ground deliberity to redevelop.

5. Human Action:

Individual Action takes place in a situation in which:

Social change is brought about by an individual.

Charisma, not the perfume, is used to describe a person who:

can charm others.

Collective Behavior involves:

A large group in non-routine behavior.

    - civil rights

Crowd occurs when:

group in same area engaging in collective behavior.

Mass is created when:

Several large groups in different locations.

Social Movements:

CHAPTER 14

The Social Institutions

In an earlier chapter we traced the evolution of societies, from the very simple Hunters and Gatherers to the very complex Post Industrial nations. We noted then, that as societies got more complex, they needed additional institutions to effectively meet the needs of its members. We also noted how important it is to understand that these institutions are closely interrelated and that a change in one will trigger changes in the others. With that reminder, let's take a closer look at the key functions of these social institutions.

The Family

Definition: Individuals related by blood, marriage, or adoption.

Key Functions

- ◇ Regulates human sexual behavior;
- ◇ Provides for the care and nurturing of infants;
- ◇ Serves as a primary agent of socialization;
- ◇ Acts as a means of social control;
- ◇ Confers status on its members.

Family Structure

- ◇ Nuclear Family

Immediate Family.
Mom, dad, siblings.

◇   **Extended Family**

Several generations living in
one home.

Creating a Family

◇   Endogamy

~~Fille~~ marrieing in one's own
group
(en - in)

◇   Exogamy

marring outside group.
(ex out)

◇   Homogamy

marrying n own social
class.

Family Process

◇   **Family of Orientation**

Family your born with

◇   **Family of Procreation**

Family you make and
marry into.

Marital Arrangements

◇   Monogamy—One spouse at a time

AMERICAN way.
one man - one woman

◇   Polygamy—A man or woman who has several spouses at same the time.
❏   Polygyny—A man who has multiple wives at the same time.

❏   Polyandry—A woman who has multiple husbands at the same time.

When you marry, husbands
brothers become yours.

◇   Serial Monogamy—Multiple remarriages

marrying, divorcing and
Remarrying.

The Future of the Family

◇   Continued increase in single-parent families;
◇   Increased legalization of same sex marriages;
◇   Continued increase in couples living together without being married (Cohabitation).

Education

Definition: Process by which a society transmits knowledge, skills, values, and norms from one generation to the next.

Key Functions

◇   Serves as a key agent of socialization;
◇   Prepares individuals for the workforce;

◇   Assists in the acquisition of wealth;

◇   Enhances social development.

Key Terms

◇   Credentialism

higher levels of education to get the same Job.

◇   Educational Attainment

number of years completed.

◇   Educational Achievement

ability to read, write, math.

◇   Tracking

placed on path vocational or acedemic

◇   Self-fulfilling Prophecy

living up to others expectations.

◇   Multicultural Education

teaching other cultures and ethnicities.

Religion

Definition: A system of beliefs and practices that address the meaning of human existence.

Key Functions

◇   Serves as a primary agent of socialization;

◇   Promotes social cohesion;

◇   Serves as a means of social control;

◇   Provides meaning and purpose to human existence.

Key Terms

◇   Theism: Worship of a supreme being or many supreme beings.

❑   Monotheism—Worship of one god.

Catholics, Jews.

◇   Polytheism—Worship of many gods.

budhisum

◇   Profane (secular)

every day things - not sacred.

◇   Sacred

thing set aside for worship.

◇   Secularization

Something that was once sacred is now secular.

◇   **Cults**

*religous group not regarded
as established religon.*

Politics—Government

Definition: People and organizations that formulate and implement public policy.

Key Functions

◇   Maintains law and order;

◇   Prevents chaos;

◇   Provides for orderly settlement of disputes;

◇   Protects citizens from foreign powers;

◇   Provides needed public services (infrastructure).

Key Terms

◇   Power—The ability to get one's way even against other people's wishes.

◇   Authority—Legitimate power.

◇   Dictatorship—One person rule.

◇   Democracy—Government for and by the people.

◇   Interest Groups (PACs)

_____

POLITICAL ACTION COMITTEES.

_____

◇   Lobbying

_____

individuals hired to influence politicians
on behalf of intrest groups.

_____

Economics

Definition: The study of the production, distribution, and consumption of goods and services.

Key Functions

◇   Creates goods and services (production);
◇   Allocates created goods and services to the members in a society (distribution);
◇   Promotes the accumulation and use of goods and services (consumption).

Key Terms

◉   Capitalism—Private ownership vs. public ownership.

capitalism is never a POLITICAl
System only economic

_____

◇   Market Economy—Supply and demand determine the prices of goods and services.

_____

_____

◇   Socialism—Public ownership vs. private ownership.

_____

_____

◇   Mixed Economy—Combines features of public and private ownership.

_____

_____

_____

◇   Transnational Corporations (multinational corporations)—An organization headquartered in one country but operates in several other countries.

_____

_____

_____

◇   Global Economy—The ability to buy and sell goods all over the world.

_____

_____

_____

Science and Technology

Definition: The process of acquiring and converting knowledge into practical uses.

Key Functions
◇   Promotes understanding of the world around us;
◇   Develops a body of knowledge to serve as the basis of action;
◇   Produces tools for use in everyday life.

Key Terms
◇   Pure Research—The search for knowledge for the purpose of knowing.

Because we want to know

◇   Applied Research—The search for knowledge in order to put it to practical use. (Technology)

Results in Technology.

_____

Health and Medicine

◇   Maintenance of Health—(Prevention)

_____

_____

_____

◇   Treatment of Illnesses—(Cure)

_____

_____

_____

◇   Extension of Life

_____

_____

_____

◇   Hypertrophy—(Dysfunctional Complexity)

tech & machines have become
more important than patients

_____